A STRANGE ROUTINE

A STRANGE ROUTINE

Tony Flynn

BLOODAXE
BOOKS

ISBN: 0 906427 20 7 (ordinary edition)
       0 906427 21 5 (signed edition of
                    25 numbered copies)

First published 1980 by
Bloodaxe Books
1 North Jesmond Avenue
Jesmond
Newcastle upon Tyne NE2 3JX

The publisher acknowledges the financial assistance
of Northern Arts and West Midlands Arts

Acknowledgements are due to the editors of the
following magazines and anthologies in which some
of these poems have appeared: *Ambit, Encounter, The
Honest Ulsterman, London Magazine, New Poetry 4* (Arts
Council/Hutchinson, 1978), *The New Review, Poetry
Review, The Poet's Yearbook* (1979), and *Stand*; some also
appeared in a pamphlet, *Separations* (Proem Pamphlets,
1976), and some were included in a collection which
was given an Eric Gregory Award in 1977.
    The author wishes to thank West Midlands Arts for
a Literature Bursary in 1977, which made possible the
writing of some of these poems.

Typesetting by Graphic Design Workshop, Newcastle
upon Tyne.

Printed in Great Britain by
Unwin Brothers Limited, Old Woking, Surrey.

For Sally

Contents

Town

(for my mother and father)

Stone quarries monument the sky
above a town still run
by men who own the mills.

My brother died here –
that is cut
in stone

at the bottom of a hill:
Francis Flynn,
aged four days.

My mother tells
of how an Irish nurse
just saved his soul,

baptising him in hospital
with water
from some flowers

by the bed. My father
carried the coffin
alone, cradled in his arms

against the rain,
soft pattering on wood –
Tonight, he woke again, listening . . .

Men, my age
at school, could give me years
today: living here

did this to them.
It is their children's eyes
that are familiar; their smiles

I remember widening
at four o'clock
on summer afternoons,

the school bell
signalling our freedom
to roam the streets they never left.

Children look
and cannot know me;
their fathers glance

then turn away.
There is a life to live,
here, and it is theirs.

Morning

Fog nuzzles our curtained window,
faint sun delights the panes.

A thin cat is scavenging the yard,
negotiating broken glass

to sniff a rotten apple.
Eyelids flick and guillotine our dreams.

4.00pm

Cars crawl away
from ticking meters.

A streetlamp
blinks like a raw eye — comes on,

floating an orange
moon in the gutter.

Office-blocks and hotels sail
above the city's distempered zoo,

and swans glide
down its poisoned canals.

The Step

Loom-deafened old women
mouth their gossip
across the street and
kneel to whiten steps –
stockings tourniquet
a wave of fat
above the knee. And they remember
when this was more
than eccentricity; when this
was a measure of respectability:
genuflections to a hard god.

Tonight

Young women are pushing prams
through sunlight.
Their pale legs flicker
like white flames
in and out of shade.

Tonight they will remember
how cool
their shadows were;
how their children's eyes
opened in them.

Citizens

Long avenue of cool trees,
these fine buildings and splendid
parks; this city
that casts its shadow
like a threat upon our heads.

In forgotten places, from
derelict kitchens and wild
gardens, our songs, subversive, Latin
and profane, rise in the night –

Around low fires
the dead and their unborn begin to dream.

Philanthropist

Their children eat out of our hands –
such beautiful young mouths
nuzzling our wrists.
                        When lips
snag on my jet ring
their blood flecks small grey teeth.

It is delicious: their skinny tongues
shivering on painted nails, our perfumed
fingertips.

Photograph

Twelve or thirteen I think
you said you were,
perched on that rock, posing
like a forties pin-up, your toes
curled
enticingly
along an edge.

Thick towels wait
to hug your legs.

Your father's Kodak
caught you like this
somewhere in Wales,
holidaying with mum and dad
for the last time.
I wonder if
they saw
your woman's smile
begin to open expertly,
your head
testing its seductive tilt,
your costume tightening.

Behind you the sea
is frozen in a calm deceit.

After Mass

Sweet candle-smoke wreathed
the Virgin's

blue smile, and incense
sickened the air.

Behind the old mill? Theresa hissed,
as we dipped our fingers together into

the cold stone font
and blessed ourselves.

Girl on a Swing, 10.00pm

A cold wind streamed her hair,
unravelling the braid she wears for school;

and her forehead shone
in the distant glow from the motorway.

A deserted park, an empty swing,
and I remember how
as she walked past me towards the gates
I caught sight of her small school badge:

a heart, a wreath of thorns, Latin
circling her breast.

Memento

The small, white, porcelain
milk jug on the table
in my room is empty. All the flowers,
leaves and ferns
you filled it with
on your last night here
shrivelled in a few days.

Dry stems cracked
and one by one I watched
soft petals stiffen
and fall, collecting
on an open book.

I have them even now
pressed between the covers of that book,
frail cameos that print
their colours on the facing page –
a graze of violet when the light shines through.

The Outhouse at My Parents' House

I prize the latch and we
step inside—Damp patches
map the whitewashed walls and
rotting beams sweeten
the air.
          My daughter lifts
a jam-jar to the light and squints
boss-eyed through its grimy glass –
'Look carefully,' I say. 'The tiny bones
of sticklebacks
I caught once, then forgot.'

Sarah! Sarah!
Sarah come quick! . .
Already bored, she dashes out
as soon as she hears the kids next door,
and scrambles over the garden fence, leaping into
their frantic game.

Why call her back? . .

For a few
fir-cones? A polished
skull? The aquarium where every spring
my frog-spawn greyed to cloudy slime?

Deserters

Traffic lulls, and blue light falls
on quiet fields behind the house.
Upstairs, the children sleep, and dream.
They have deserted us; now
they abandon each other.

Patrick's tiny footprints
zigzag across endless
white sands.

Sarah, crouched
in mud, is talking to
a fat black slug
on the palm of her floating hand.

Separation

Miles away you nurse
a small and
complicated head
against your breast.
All night
my mind is pounding trains
along the lines between us.

Growing

You are the child
I left behind. Two years older
than when I saw you last . . .
Apart, we grow old
together, through the same years.
At least our two hearts beat
a harmony in this.
                    But you are right,
it is no consolation.
To be in the same world
is not so much.

Departure

Ready to leave, released
from vows
to watch our children
run their childhood through
these rooms we've cleared
of everything –
their clutter of permanence
boxed and ready for
our separate destinations.
Your name is strange
in block capitals
on the label of your trunk;
hard and isolate, insisting
you are you –
so much must be wrong
for this to shock so terribly.
Your new address
printed below
is already more real
than here—I let my mind run
brick by brick
along the streets
you'll live between alone.
Our bed, stripped to a cold frame,
a headboard and a base,
refutes my memories –
love is not dismantled
half so easily as this.

Wedding Portrait

Three years later,
divorced, I found my wedding portrait
in my mother's house,
stored in a small box.
The only other content
their first-born, my dead brother's
birth certificate. Two anniversaries
whittled to a quick look on the day.

Daughter
(for Sarah)

From her bedroom window she watches the snow:
wind hauls bare trees against the house
and a sycamore scrawls on icy panes.
Her lilac-bush shivers its soft white fringe.

When the day is still
she trails from room to room,
gazing alone into a sky
where snow clouds drift away from her.

The Alarm

Her children have their children.
They are the laughing families
crowding the hot compartments
of holiday trains.

She watches the hours
circle themselves
in the face of her clock.
At ten
she winds the alarm
and thinks
of the one morning
she will not hear it ring.

A Mother's Death

Night, and your frail
plants exhaust our air.
                    In the washing-basket
soiled clothes accumulate.
Soon they will spill
into the room
and life will begin again –
they will wash their own socks.

Wristwatch

Stopped clocks
intimidate: still hands, a portent
at whatever hour, set her fingers scurrying across
her wrist's blue bracelet
of veins to touch
the jewelled precision there.
                           A tiny pulse
quickens under ticking glass.

The Search

We peered from an upstairs window,
breath fogging the glass
above dim kitchens and narrow
streets, but could only hear
our lost dog
whining out there, the far side
of bleary, orange lights.

I searched dark fields
to trace its cry—cold blades of grass
surprised my thin, bare legs.
Alone, beyond
familiar haunts,
I learnt to risk
my hands where my eyes failed.

Sunday

Old women fingering their hard, black beads;
the muttering faithful, Aves to the Virgin,
    whisperings,
bronchial wheezing at the altar rail.
Hands tighten on a crucifix and cut
its Christ into a woman's palm.

Young communicants, we offered our tongues.
Bowed head and downcast eyes –
feigned submissions, then the bite:
hosts crushed between our teeth.
Altar wine we stole
was never turned to blood
in our thieving mouths—the old priest's threat –
but sweet on our breath as we walked home
to fruit cake on best china plates
and silence over stiff, white tablecloths.

Myth

At birth a full moon lit my fontanel;
Mother smiled, and watched the soft pulse
beat. My afterbirth she shredded through
the branches of an apple-tree: no fruit

or blossom's graced a bough since then.
Let this be my last will and testament:
a mound of earth, unmarked, a crow-haven
among the suicides, the mad, the poor.

Jessica Drew's Married Son

Where streetlamps burn
their orange glare
through windows into rooms –
into a room;

by the bed a tattered
Roman missal, above it a bleeding Sacred Heart;

and Jessica Drew, five-days-dead,
is staring from her cold grey sheets
over dark roofs
and rain-drenched fields,

through centrally heated
air and through
his wife's blue chiffon evening-dress,

down the long curve
of his sleeping spine.

Penalties

I remember
winter evenings in the big house, and you
intense, inventing terrible penalties
for superstitions crossed—a broken mirror
might leave us
pox-marked or dumb, paralysed for ever
to stare at the ceiling.

Mother smiled, and called you
her little old woman –
                              This afternoon
we are both
old.
    As we shuffle slowly
arm in arm
along gravel paths that all lead back
to your locked
ward, you draw me close
and trembling
confess: 'The door
I left ajar . . . Mother's black glove
that I haven't touched
for twenty minutes now . . .'

O my poor
love, what else
exacts
this weeping under sweet laburnums?

Letters

Tightening her grip on the grey-blue sheets
of paper as limp as drowned leaves, my mother read
her sister to us.
               And mumbling lines
that trembled her, would snap
'Just listen!' whenever I asked
what it was she'd said that we hadn't caught.

But still awake at ten one night,
in the small room next to our parents' room,
we heard the rest of Aunt Ivy's news
through stifled tears my father hushed—*I strangled
old Lizzie's tabby cat—the one
that used to prowl the ward—and hid the body
behind a bush. The head
I've kept
for its eyes.*

The locked drawer where the letters were
was at last too much to resist—I slipped the key
from under the clock . . .

One crumpled page began
in something like my mother's hand, impossible
to understand—I blamed
the adult style. And then
what looked like my
'real writing': I stared and made
nothing of it.

Her brother went
to see her there, and sat
and watched
something he had known
evaporate through eyes
professionally dimmed
to hide her rage.

We only got the letters.
In the last one,
her name was a thin line
that straggled off the page.

Recluse

Smoking the hours. Fag-ends litter
the tabletop, ash on my shirt
and trousers, on the few books
I still possess, and never read.
It is their smell I've come to love:
the yellowed page I lift to my face
and breathe. Poems, stories, all

long forgotten; but brackish print,
the smoke-scent of a first edition . . .
I close my eyes, and live.
I do not know or care what time it is.
Days fly through me
like grey sea birds through mist
on their way to the sea.

Her Room

Waking to watch familiar shadows creep
across the flowered carpet of her room,
worn roses and the faded bloom
that she alone has trodden down,
her colours that she walks upon . . .

She knows exactly where
each shadow's edge will fall,
then how it falls from there
back to its object in the room.
On certain days she hears it all,
like breath; her bed, her chair,
exhaling through the silent air
their own dark shapes, her things.

Burning Leaves

Hungry gulls,
blown inland by rough
sea winds, scavenge
above the rambling grounds,
and circle
a bonfire of leaves.

Smoke drifts
from the lawn
into her hair, ash
flecks her throat and
settles
on a pillow.

She dreams herself
into the flames
where a thousand bright
tongues all play at her feet;

and the hissing embers
whisper her name.

The First Day

Fingers worry fingers
in her lap all afternoon,

creasing her flowered dress.
The white ghosts drift

from behind their glass,
efficient, smiling

quietly at her. One
takes her arm, and leads the way

to her room. Black pools at last
eclipse her eyes . . .

She turns, looks up—the small
high window's

long needle of light
is blue, and fastens her gaze.

A Strange Routine

Rooms fascinate: a white rocking-chair,
empty picture-frames, a glass of water
left beside the bed, mirrors reflecting
a vase, and then the vase . . .
Ghosts of conversation hush to my step.
Goldfish darken in their bowl:
it's time I changed the water, time
I fed them; time I watered his plants.
A strange routine, a temporary lodging.
I sleep in another man's bed, naked
between his sheets, dreaming on his pillow.
I perform his small duties about the place.
The street below me is familiar, but
not from here, not looking down
like this; listening to traffic, uneasy,
its constant drone. At night I wake
beside a woman, and she, turning, calls me from a
    dream.

Sleep, sleep my love . . .
His accent on my words assuring her.

Interior

A rubber-plant
by the open window
can hear, as you will never
hear, rain
on a derelict roof
falling in forgotten rooms;
the low mourning
of distant generators.
And knows, as you do not,
the suffering of clocks,
of wristwatch, pocket-watch,
forever circling
the same still hours.

Oranges

On the table by the small
grey window
a bunch of keys, a toothbrush,
spectacles.

Take them and draw
the blue
flowered curtains;

lock all the doors,
and leave.

I have decided
to sit it out
here, let my teeth
rot, and live
on oranges—my tongue working
the soft
quarters, my eyes
open, blind.

When the Others Are Away

We are alone in the house;
everyone else away visiting parents
or the coast for a few days.
We indulge our run of the place –
you in your bath
with the door open wide;
wandering back into the flat
naked and excited, imagining eyes
follow your wet prints
on the floor. I sit on the stairs.
I could sit here, if I wished,
for at least
three days, and no one
would tread on me. We dream
from room to room—cold light
on an empty vase . . . old letters
hidden in a drawer; bric-a-brac of lives
we thought they'd locked away.

She Talks to Herself

Another year, greening
through a gentle rain
to this,
the long year's end:
an apple-tree
offering the sky
apples.

Already it is too cold
to feed the birds in my dressing-gown:
most have left
or do not fly
to where crumbs fall from shrivelled
hands—dead leaves
nagged
by the wind.

Soon there will be snow.
Then I will count the flakes; listening
to the vicious tick
in my antique clock,
to the sour chimes
of my own voice
counting.

Ice cracks in the garden.
It is like the sound of small
white bones
crushed somewhere in the night . . .

Poem

Incense in the children's hair
an hour after Mass.

Rosary beads, a black
Latin missal, crumpled soft
white cotton gloves . . .

And is this you
about to lift
the wooden bowl your father carved?

Are you the girl
who offers me

the darkest peach I've ever seen?

The New Dress

Undressing, her fingers find the zip,
and small teeth open along her spine.
She shivers, and can't resist
her mirror—the thrill as the blue
falls from her. She remembers
her cats . . . how their slack lope
bodies a cruel deceit—slit eyes
in the long grass, patient, murderous.
She dreams again the measured glide
of claw, the silent puncture's tiny bleb
of red at feathered throats—such skill.
She purrs, and steps from her silky pool.

Mirror

Her hands cup
and lift each breast
a little higher

He watches
from the bed

When she
turns
he will close
his eyes for her

She turns
before the mirror floats
its beautiful corpse
against the glass

The Bookshop

Your name on the fly-leaf of a book
I borrowed, above the date: Easter, '76.
A year ago, and I was with you
then, in our favourite bookshop
where we talked and smoked with friends:
old hippies still mumbling 'far out';
bored social workers come to kill
an hour—their young offenders locked
in sober-coloured cars outside;
the odd dope-fiend; the few
who wanted books for Eng. Lit. courses.

Shelves of Sci-Fi, Penguins, poetry,
and *How to Grow Your Own*, where
fish once lay on cold, white slabs.

You browsed, then seized upon
another Russian monster. How you loved
those dark passions—malevolence
bearded and brooding, peasants
stinking of stolen vodka—and you
nineteen, petite, and Welsh.

Hopper's American Hotel Rooms

Sunlight on bare walls
and the single bed

Three brown suitcases

on each
a square label

blank
no name
no address

A blue Ford
is parked outside
the small hotel

and the tyres
are warm

Four o'clock
in the afternoon
summer 1931

Nothing
happens

Sunlight on
bare walls and
one suitcase

Nothing is about
to happen

Foreigners

They live upstairs on the second floor –
Kashia, Piotr, and their great-grandmother.
When the old woman strays
from the house on her own, neighbours
always know where to find her—slumped
on a bench in the derelict
station, gazing down
the overgrown lines. Kashia has grey eyes and long
skinny arms. Her little brother
could steal your shadow. I've seen him in
Brierley's corner-shop, thieving
comics and crisps, oranges, fags . . . But it's
oranges mostly he can't resist,
and loves to eat
crouched on the sill of his bedroom window,
spitting the pips in a high arc
over the fence into next door's garden.
Kashia pretends not to see him, and smiles.
One day, she thinks, *an orange-tree might blossom*
there, and they'll have Piotr to thank.

The Fish

After making love
in your attic flat
on a mattress
that cushions the bare
floorboards, you seemed
at ease, and talked
about the fish you'd watched
that afternoon—a trout, you thought,
in the stream
behind the old mill.

'It dozed by the bank
for hours, so still
it might have been dead. But so
perfectly still, against
the flow, it had to be alive,' you said.

Then you fell asleep
for the first time in months
without booze or the usual
pills, and hardly
moved until I felt
you edge from my arms in tears.

Dreaming, did you
dip your hand
to touch a stillness
under water,
and touching
water
dart a fish?

Schiele in Prison

There are bars across my small sky.
Light that shines between them stands
in columns on the wall above my bed.

I watch a seagull rise
behind them; it hangs in the blue air
then lifts

effortlessly away. In the forest
sap is rising, it is Spring –
the first flowers, the singing of small birds

with shining eyes. In the city
my room gathers its perfect light
into a mirror

that is cold and clear, like a pool
in the forest after rain. And women came
like sleek cats out of that light

into my mirror's light;
and were beautiful there, cruel,
elegant, and beautiful. Now they are gone –

back to their snoring husbands,
to their madames, back
to their lives.

And I am a snail
listening to the grey sea
echo in my shell, counting

the distant tides;
dreaming of birds
that will come at last

with sharp beaks
to pluck out my eyes,
carrying bits of me to everywhere.

Note on the Artist

Dave Livingstone was born in 1951 in Glasgow. He studied at Stirling University, Loughborough College of Education and Coventry Polytechnic; he was a semi-professional musician in a folk band for three years, and is now a social worker. His watercolours have been shown in two one-man exhibitions; he is currently writing and illustrating a story about a tribe of "gnomadic" gnomes. He lives in Huncote, Leicestershire. Enquiries to Enderby Crafts, c/o Denis & Glenda Humphreys, 11 Mill Hill, Enderby, Leics (tel: Leicester 866810).